Playing witl
Presen
Shakespea

Romeo & Juliet
FOR KIDS

(The melodramatic version!)

For 6-18+ actors, or kids of all ages who want to have fun!
Creatively modified by
Brendan P. Kelso
Cover illustrations by
Shana Hallmeyer and Ron Leishman

3 Melodramatic Modifications of Shakespeare's Play
for 3 different group sizes:

6-11

9-13

14-18+

Table Of Contents

To Mom & Dad;
Without their support I would have never, well, everything!

-Brendan

For performance rights please see page 6 of this book or contact:

contact@PlayingWithPlays.com

Foreword

When I was in high school there was something about Shakespeare that appealed to me. Not that I understood it mind you, but there were clear scenes and images that always stood out in my mind. Romeo & Juliet, "Romeo, Romeo; wherefore art thou Romeo?"; Julius Caesar, "Et tu Brute"; Macbeth, "Double, Double, toil and trouble"; Hamlet, "to be or not to be"; A Midsummer Night's Dream, all I remember about this was a wickedly cool fairy and something about a guy turning into a donkey that I thought was pretty funny. It was not until I started analyzing Shakespeare's plays as an actor that I realized one very important thing, I still didn't understand them. Seriously though, it's tough enough for adults, let alone kids. Then it hit me, why don't I make a version that kids could perform, but make it easy for them to understand with a splash of Shakespeare lingo mixed in? And voila! A melodramatic masterpiece was created! They are intended to be melodramatically fun!

THE PLAYS: There are 3 plays within this book, for three different group sizes. The reason: to allow educators or parents to get the story across to their children regardless of the size of their group. As you read through the plays, there are several lines that are highlighted. These are actual lines from the original book. I am a little more particular about the kids saying these lines verbatim. But the rest, well... have fun!

The entire purpose of this book is to instill the love of a classic story, as well as drama, into the kids.

And when you have children who have a passion for something, they will start to teach themselves, with or without school.

These plays are intended for pure fun. Please DO NOT have the kids learn these lines verbatim, that would be a complete waste of creativity. But do have them basically know their lines and improvise wherever they want as long as it pertains to telling the story. Because that is the goal of an actor: to tell the story. In A Midsummer Night's Dream, I once had a student playing Quince question me about one of her lines, "but in the actual story, didn't the Mechanicals state that 'they would hang us'?" I thought for a second and realized that she had read the story with her mom, and she was right. So I let her add the line she wanted and it added that much more fun, it made the play theirs. I have had kids throw water on the audience, run around the audience, sit in the audience, lose their pumpkin pants (size 30 around a size 15 doesn't work very well, but makes for some great humor!) and most importantly, die all over the stage. The kids love it.

One last note: if you want some educational resources, loved our plays, want to tell the world how much your kids loved performing Shakespeare, want to insult someone with our Shakespeare Insult Generator, or are just a fan of Shakespeare, then hop on our website and have fun:

PlayingWithPlays.com

With these notes, I'll see you on the stage, have fun, and break a leg!

SCHOOL, AFTERSCHOOL, and SUMMER classes

I've been teaching these plays as afterschool and summer programs for quite some time. Many people have asked what the program is, therefore, I have put together a basic formula so any teacher or parent can follow and have melodramatic success! As well, many teachers use my books in a variety of ways. You can view the formula and many more resources on my website at: PlayingWithPlays.com

ROYALTIES

I am asked all the time about royalties for my plays. So, here are the basic rules:

1) Please contact me! I always LOVE to hear about a school or group performing my books!

2) If you are a group and DO NOT charge your kids to be in this production: contact me, and we can talk about waiving the book costs or discounts on signed copies.

3) If you are a group and DO NOT charge the audience to see the plays, there is no royalty! (but, please leave a positive review, and send some photos!)

4) If you are a group and DO charge your kids to be in the production, contact me as I will give you a bulk discount (8 books or more), sign each book, and send some really cool press on Shakespeare tattoos!

5) If you are a group and DO charge the audience to see the performance, please contact me to discuss royalty options.

Any other questions or comments, please email me at:

contact@PlayingWithPlays.com

The 15-Minute or so Romeo & Juliet
By William Shakespeare
Creatively modified by
Brendan P. Kelso
6-11 Actors

THE CAPULETS
JULIET – The Babe (but a Capulet)
NURSE – Juliet's lifelong Nurse
[2]**TYBALT** – Juliet's cousin

THE MONTAGUES
[3]**ROMEO** – The Dude (but a Montague)
[1]**BENVOLIO** – Romeo's friend
[4]**BALTHASAR** – Romeo's servant

THE COURT
[3]**PRINCE ESCALES** – the local Prince
[4]**MERCUTIO** – Romeo's friend
[4]**PARIS** – Wants to marry Juliet

THE CHURCH
[1]**FRIAR LAWRENCE** – A friar that helps
[2]**FRIAR JOHN** – A friar that doesn't help

The same actors can play the following parts:

[1]FRIAR LAWRENCE and BENVOLIO
[2]TYBALT and FRIAR JOHN
[3]ROMEO and the PRINCE
[4]BALTHASAR, MERCUTIO, and PARIS

PROLOGUE

(Montagues enter on one side of stage and face audience in a line and say, "Montagues" then they stand back; Capulets enter from the other side of the stage and say, "Capulets" then they stand back; they briefly glare, growl, and yell at each other; they then form a semi-circle and address the audience)

ROMEO: Two households, both alike in dignity,

JULIET: In fair Verona, where we lay our scene,

FRIAR LAWRENCE: From ancient grudge break to new mutiny,

TYBALT: Where civil blood makes civil hands unclean.

MERCUTIO: From forth the fatal loins of these two foes

NURSE: A pair of star-cross'd lovers take their life

BENVOLIO: Whose misadventured piteous overthrows

BALTHASAR: Doth with their death bury their parents' strife.

PRINCE: The fearful passage of their death-marked love,

PARIS: And the continuance of their parents' rage,

FRIAR JOHN: Which but their children's end, nought could remove,

TYBALT: Is now the two hours', achmmm....15 minutes', traffic of our stage;

MERCUTIO: The which if you with patient ears attend,

NURSE: What here shall miss, our toil shall strive to mend. *(ALL exit)*

ACT 1 SCENE 1

(enter BENVOLIO)

BENVOLIO: Man, I am tired of all this fighting over Capulets and Montagues. Throughout my entire life, I have learned to hate Capulets. But there has been so much fighting that I think I am going to take the summer off.

(enter TYBALT)

TYBALT: What? A Montague? You want to fight! Let's go!

(wanting to fight)

BENVOLIO: *(drawing his sword)* Do you bite your thumb at me, sir?

TYBALT: I do bite my thumb, sir. Bring it on!

BENVOLIO: Whoa, we really shouldn't be fighting. Put down your sword. *(aside)* Not like you know what to do with it anyway. I do but keep the peace.

TYBALT: What! Drawn and talk of peace? I hate the word, as I hate hell, all Montagues, and thee. Have at thee coward!

(they fight; PRINCE enters)

PRINCE: Rebellious subjects, enemies to peace. Will they not hear? *(as loud as possible)* STOP!!!!!! *(they all stop and go to their appropriate side)* This is the third time this year you have caused a riot on MY streets, and I am really getting tired of it. If ever you disturb our streets again, your lives shall pay the forfeit of the peace. Clear?

ALL: Clear.

TYBALT: Ahhhh, sorry but it's not clear to me, and probably not clear to them. *(points at audience)* I don't understand.

PRINCE: If you start a fight again, I will kill you – Clear? *(TYBALT nods)* Good, now, on pain of death, all men depart. *(no one leaves)* Go! *(ALL exit except BENVOLIO)*

BENVOLIO: Whew, I am glad that fighting is over. Now, where is Romeo, his mother wants me to look after him because he has been acting rather strange lately.

(ROMEO enters)

BENVOLIO: Romeo, Romeo!

ROMEO: Benvolio, there is this really cool girl, Rosaline, I mean, she's cute! Anyway, I like her a lot. But she wants nothing to do with me, what do I do?

BENVOLIO: Don't worry about her, there are other fish in the sea.

ROMEO: Yeah, whatever. Then teach me how I should forget to think. But hey, I hear she is going to a big party tonight, should we go?

BENVOLIO: Yes, and I will show you other girls more beautiful than she. Like her! Right there in the audience! *(points at audience member)* And I will make thee think thy swan a crow.

ROMEO: You're on!

(ALL exit)

ACT 1 SCENE 2

(PARIS enters and addresses audience)

PARIS: Hello, I'm Paris! I just asked Lord Capulet if I could marry his daughter, Juliet. He was a little upset and said something about her being only 13; just a kid; not ready for marriage; she can't even drive yet; blah, blah, blah..... Anyway, he said they are having a party tonight and if she likes me he will approve of our marriage! Awesome!

(PARIS exits)

ACT 1 SCENE 3

(enter NURSE and JULIET)

NURSE: I hear that Paris thinks you are really cute. You know, I have been your nurse all your life Juliet, and I believe you should think about marrying this guy, because he is very good looking.

JULIET: If I like him, I will think about it.

NURSE: Great! Hey, let's go to the party!

(ALL exit)

ACT 1 SCENE 4

(enter ROMEO, MERCUTIO, BENVOLIO wearing masks)

BENVOLIO: Mercutio, are you sure that by wearing these masks we will be safe at a Capulet party?

MERCUTIO: No problem, they will have no clue.

ROMEO: Well, here we are. But I don't see Rosaline.

BENVOLIO: I told you, look at the other girls.

ROMEO: Yeah, yeah.

MERCUTIO: You need to laugh my friend, if love be rough with you; be rough with love.

ROMEO: Leave me alone.

(enter JULIET, TYBALT, NURSE, and other maskers all dancing and having a fun time)

ROMEO: *(seeing Juliet for the first time)* What lady is that which doth enrich the hand of yonder knight?

MERCUTIO: No clue, man.

ROMEO: *(to himself)* O she doth teach the torches to burn bright!

TYBALT: *(noticing Romeo)* What a Montague in the house of Capulet? Ohhh, if my Lord wasn't right there, I would pick a fight with him. Aghhhh.... I will get him later.

(TYBALT exits)

ROMEO: *(to Juliet)* Hey you're cute.

JULIET: So are you.

NURSE: Juliet, your mother wants to talk with you.

ROMEO: Who is her mother?

NURSE: Lady Capulet.

ROMEO: *(very dramatic to audience)* Oh nooooo. My mom is going to be bummed. I just fell in love with a Capulet. *(ROMEO exits)*

JULIET: Nurse, who was that?

NURSE: Romeo, a Montague.

JULIET: *(very dramatic to audience)* Uh oh, that's trouble. I just fell in love with a Montague.

(ALL exit)

ACT 2 SCENE 1

(enter ROMEO and JULIET)

ROMEO: *(seeing JULIET)* But, soft! What light through yonder window breaks? It is the east, and Juliet is the sun.

JULIET: Ay me!

ROMEO: *(overwhelmed by her words)* She speaks! O speak again, bright angel!

JULIET: O Romeo, Romeo! Wherefore art thou Romeo? Deny thy father and refuse thy name; Or if thou wilt not, be but sworn my love, and I'll no longer be a Capulet. What's in a name? That which we call a rose by any other name would smell as sweet.

ROMEO: *(aside)* She is my sworn enemy, but look at her, WOW she's cute! See, how she leans her cheek upon her hand! O that I were a glove upon that hand, that I might touch that cheek! *(ROMEO is in a daze)*

JULIET: O Romeo, Romeo! Hello! HEY ROMEO!

ROMEO: Oh yeah, sorry, just daydreaming over here. Hey, I love you.

JULIET: And I love you.

ROMEO: I got an idea, let's get married.

JULIET: Okay. I will send my nurse tomorrow to find the time and place of our marriage.

ROMEO: Cool.

NURSE: *(offstage)* Juliet!

JULIET: Good night, Good night! Parting is such sweet sorrow, that I shall say good night till it be morrow.

(JULIET exits)

ROMEO: I need to go talk to Friar Lawrence to figure out this marriage thing.

(ROMEO exits)

(enter FRIAR LAWRENCE)

FRIAR LAWRENCE: Ah, what a beautiful morning. *(picks up a plant and pricks his finger)* Ouch! Plants, like people, can be both good and evil.

(enter ROMEO)

FRIAR LAWRENCE: Romeo, what brings you here today?

ROMEO: I have a small request, and it's just slightly complicated. *(pauses)* I want to get married to Juliet.

FRIAR LAWRENCE: *(outraged)* The Capulet!

ROMEO: Yeah.

FRIAR LAWRENCE: *(still outraged)* Are you crazy!

ROMEO: But I am in love.

FRIAR LAWRENCE: *(very calm)* Well, okay. This might end the feud between the Montagues and the Capulets.

ROMEO: Awesome!

(ALL exit)

ACT 2 SCENE 3

(enter MERCUTIO and BENVOLIO)

BENVOLIO: Mercutio, have you seen Romeo since last night's party?

MERCUTIO: *(joking)* He's probably still in love with Rosaline.

(ROMEO enters)

ROMEO: Hey guys!

MERCUTIO: *(teasing Romeo)* Still in love with Rosaline?

ROMEO: Well now that you mention it ...

(enter NURSE)

NURSE: So what's the plan?

MERCUTIO: *(very sarcastic)* Hey Romeo, now she's better than Rosaline.

NURSE: *(to Romeo)* What saucy merchant was this, that was so full of himself?

ROMEO: Ignore him, he's just a gentleman that LOVES to hear himself talk. Tell Juliet we will get married this afternoon at Friar Lawrence's.

NURSE: Okay.

(ALL exit)

ACT 2 SCENE 4

(enter FRIAR LAWRENCE, ROMEO, JULIET)

JULIET: My Nurse told me to meet you here to be married.

FRIAR LAWRENCE: Are you ready?

ROMEO: Ready.

JULIET: Ready.

FRIAR LAWRENCE: Okay, all done, you're married. You can now kiss the bride.

(ROMEO and JULIET look at each other and then towards FRIAR LAWRENCE shaking their heads 'no')

FRIAR LAWRENCE: Okay, fine, you can hug.

(ROMEO and JULIET look at each other and then towards FRIAR LAWRENCE shaking their heads 'no')

FRIAR LAWRENCE: Okay, okay. Can you at least shake hands?

(ROMEO and JULIET look at each other and decide to high five instead)

FRIAR LAWRENCE: *(to audience)* They just got married! Let's hear it for them!

(FRIAR gets audience to clap; ALL exit)

ACT 3 SCENE 1

(enter BENVOLIO and MERCUTIO; enter TYBALT from opposite side)

TYBALT: *(angry)* Where's Romeo?

MERCUTIO: You want some of me?

TYBALT: No, I want Romeo.

(enter ROMEO)

ROMEO: My good friends.

TYBALT: Bring it on, Romeo. Thou art a villain.

ROMEO: I will not fight you.

MERCUTIO: *(wanting to fight)* Come on Romeo.

ROMEO: No, I have my reasons.

BENVOLIO: We should listen to Romeo.

MERCUTIO: Fine, I'll fight him.

TYBALT: Let's go!

(MERCUTIO and TYBALT fight)

ROMEO: NO!

(TYBALT stabs MERCUTIO)

ROMEO: Good Mercutio!

MERCUTIO: A plague o' both your houses. I am sped.

(MERCUTIO dies)

ROMEO: Noooooooooooo, Mercutio! Aghhh....Tybalt, I'm really upset, I mean really, REALLY upset. *(pulling his sword out)*

BENVOLIO: Whoa, Romeo. Do you see that guy? *(pointing at dead MERCUTIO)* Do you want to be like him?

TYBALT: Oh yeah!

ROMEO: Yeah!

(ROMEO and TYBALT fight, TYBALT is killed)

BENVOLIO: Romeo, away, be gone!

(ROMEO exits; PRINCE enters)

PRINCE: What in the world happened here? Why are there dead bodies on the ground all over MY streets? Huh?

BENVOLIO: Well, Tybalt killed Mercutio, and then Romeo killed Tybalt.

PRINCE: Fine, then Romeo is banished from Verona, and clean up this mess!

(BENVOLIO drags bodies off stage; ALL exit)

ACT 3 SCENE 2

(enter ROMEO and FRIAR LAWRENCE)

ROMEO: Friar, I did a bad thing.

FRIAR LAWRENCE: Yeah, I heard, not too good of you. The prince says you are to be banished from the kingdom.

ROMEO: Nooooooooooooo! I will never be able to see my Juliet again!

(ROMEO falls on the ground crying, very melodramatic; NURSE enters)

NURSE: Friar, have you seen Romeo?

(FRIAR points to the ground)

NURSE: Oh, yeah, pretty obvious and a bit pathetic. Hey lover boy. Juliet is pretty bummed.

ROMEO: Noooooooooooooo!

(ROMEO tries to stab himself, failing miserably; NURSE takes sword away)

FRIAR LAWRENCE: Why don't you go see Juliet, and then leave town.

ROMEO: *(excited)* Great idea!

(ALL exit)

ACT 4 SCENE 1

(enter ROMEO and JULIET)

JULIET: Oh Romeo!

ROMEO: Oh Juliet! It is almost morning, and I must leave.

JULIET: Do you have to?

ROMEO: I must be gone and live, or stay and die. And I really prefer the going and living thing.

(NURSE enters)

NURSE: Whoa, you're still here, you better leave soon, and when I say "soon" I mean, NOW!

(NURSE shoves out ROMEO; ROMEO exits)

NURSE: Oh, by the way, Juliet, your dad says you have to marry Paris.

JULIET: I don't want to.

NURSE: What! That is what your parents say and you better listen!

JULIET: Fine!

(NURSE exits)

JULIET: I need to talk with Friar Lawrence.

(enter FRIAR LAWRENCE)

FRIAR LAWRENCE: You called?

JULIET: I want to stay with Romeo, what can I do?

FRIAR LAWRENCE: No problem. Just take this herbal cocktail. You will look like you are dead. And when they take you to the morgue, your Romeo will be there waiting. *(calling offstage)* Friar John!

(FRIAR JOHN enters)

FRIAR JOHN: Yes.

FRIAR LAWRENCE: I need you to send a message to Romeo.

FRIAR JOHN: Okay.

(FRIAR JOHN exits)

FRIAR LAWRENCE: *(calling offstage)* FRIAR JOHN!

(FRIAR JOHN enters)

FRIAR JOHN: Yes?

FRIAR LAWRENCE: You don't know what the message is.

FRIAR JOHN: Oh. Well, what is it?

FRIAR LAWRENCE: Tell Romeo to meet Juliet at the tomb tomorrow evening.

FRIAR JOHN: Okay.

(FRIAR JOHN exits)

FRIAR LAWRENCE: Good luck.

(FRIAR LAWRENCE exits)

JULIET: To drink, or not to drink, that is the question. Well, bottoms up!

(JULIET drinks potion, and passes out; NURSE enters)

NURSE: Rise and shine my dear. Juliet? Wake up. JULIET! NOOOOOOO.

(FRIAR LAWRENCE and PARIS enter)

ALL: Aghhhhh....

FRIAR LAWRENCE: *(to himself)* Wow, that was quick.

NURSE: What?

FRIAR LAWRENCE: *(badly faking a cough)* I said, I feel sick. Now we need to take her to the tomb.

(they pick up JULIET, and carry her off stage, ALL exit)

(enter ROMEO and BALTHASAR)

ROMEO: *(very happy)* Balthasar my servant, the day is beautiful! How are you today?

BALTHASAR: Ummm, okay.

ROMEO: Only okay, but the day is beautiful!

BALTHASAR: Well sir, ummmm I have bad news. Really bad news.

ROMEO: Really, no good news?

BALTHASAR: Nope.

ROMEO: Not even just a little.

BALTHASAR: Nope, nada, and no.

ROMEO: What's the bad news?

BALTHASAR: Juliet is dead.

ROMEO: NOOOOOOO......I am going to get some poison and kill myself tonight in her tomb.

(ALL exit)

(enter FRIAR JOHN and FRIAR LAWRENCE)

FRIAR LAWRENCE: Hello Friar John, were you able to deliver the letter? What says Romeo?

FRIAR JOHN: Well, I tried, but it just didn't happen, so I got a burger and fries instead, want one?

FRIAR LAWRENCE: What! That's not good. Bad, very bad. Poor Juliet, closed in a dead man's tomb. I have to go save them!

(ALL exit)

(JULIET is lying dead on the ground, enter ROMEO)

ROMEO: I will open her tomb and kill myself next to my dear love Juliet!

(enter PARIS)

PARIS: My dear Romeo Montague, what are you doing here, disturbing a Capulet? I am putting you under arrest!

ROMEO: This is a bad time Paris. Tempt not a desperate man.

(they fight; ROMEO kills PARIS)

ROMEO: O Juliet, how I love you so. Here's to my love! *(Drinks poison)* Hmmmm, tastes like soda. *(or drink of choice)* Thus with a kiss I die.

(ROMEO dies; enter FRIAR LAWRENCE)

FRIAR LAWRENCE: Oh shoot, I am too late.

(JULIET awakes)

JULIET: O comfortable Friar, where is my lord?

FRIAR LAWRENCE: Yeah, well there was a slight problem with the plan. *(points at ground)*

JULIET: NOOOOOOOOOO!

FRIAR LAWRENCE: *(noises heard offstage)* I hear people coming, let's go!

(FRIAR LAWRENCE exits)

JULIET: No! What's here? Poison I see hath been his timeless end. Bummer, he left none for me. *(more noises outside)* Then I'll be brief. O happy dagger...

(ROMEO hands dagger to JULIET)

JULIET: Thank you. O happy dagger, this is thy sheath; there rust, and let me die.

(JULIET dies and falls on ROMEO; enter FRIAR LAWRENCE)

FRIAR LAWRENCE: *(addresses audience)* Well, I was just outside and I had to tell the prince what happened. When I told Lord Montague and Lord Capulet that their son and daughter were married, boy were they mad! But then I told them about the dead bodies here, and then they were sad. The prince then told them that this is what happens if you don't get along. And both lords agreed and decided to shake hands, hug, and live happily ever after. For never was a story of more woe, than this of Juliet and her Romeo.

(starts applauding with audience)

THE END

The 20-Minute or so
Romeo & Juliet
By William Shakespeare
Creatively modified by Brendan P. Kelso
9-13 Actors

THE CAPULETS
LORD/LADY CAPULET – Dad/Mom Capulet
JULIET – The Babe (but a Capulet)
NURSE – Juliet's lifelong Nurse
[2]**TYBALT** – Juliet's cousin

THE MONTAGUES
LORD/LADY MONTAGUE – Dad/Mom Montague
ROMEO – The Dude (but a Montague)
[1]**BENVOLIO** – Romeo's friend
[3]**BALTHASAR** – Romeo's servant

THE COURT
[3]**PRINCE ESCALES** – the local Prince
[4]**MERCUTIO** – Romeo's friend
[4]**PARIS** – Wants to marry Juliet

THE CHURCH
[1]**FRIAR LAWRENCE** – A friar that helps
[2]**FRIAR JOHN** – A friar that doesn't help

The same actors can play the following parts:

[1]BENVOLIO and FRIAR LAWRENCE
[2]TYBALT and FRIAR JOHN
[3]PRINCE and BALTHASAR
[4]MERCUTIO and PARIS

PROLOGUE

(Montagues enter on one side of stage and face audience in a line and say, "Montagues" then they stand back; Capulets enter from the other side of the stage and say, "Capulets" then they stand back; they briefly glare, growl, and yell at each other; they then form a semi-circle and address the audience)

ROMEO: Two households, both alike in dignity,

JULIET: In fair Verona, where we lay our scene,

FRIAR LAWRENCE: From ancient grudge break to new mutiny,

TYBALT: Where civil blood makes civil hands unclean.

MERCUTIO: From forth the fatal loins of these two foes

NURSE: A pair of star-cross'd lovers take their life

LORD/LADY CAPULET: Whose misadventured piteous overthrows

LORD/LADY MONTAGUE: Doth with their death bury their parents' strife.

BENVOLIO: The fearful passage of their death-marked love,

BALTHASAR: And the continuance of their parents' rage,

PRINCE: Which but their children's end, nought could remove,

FRIAR JOHN: Is now the two hours', achmmm....20 minutes', traffic of our stage;

PARIS: The which if you with patient ears attend,

NURSE: What here shall miss, our toil shall strive to mend.

(ALL exit)

ACT 1 SCENE 1

(enter BENVOLIO)

BENVOLIO: Man, I am tired of all this fighting over Capulets and Montagues. Throughout my entire life, I have learned to hate Capulets. But there has been so much fighting that I think I am going to take the summer off.

(enter TYBALT)

TYBALT: What? A Montague? You want to fight! Let's go!

(wanting to fight)

BENVOLIO: *(drawing his sword)* Do you bite your thumb at me, sir?

TYBALT: I do bite my thumb, sir. Bring it on!

BENVOLIO: Whoa, we really shouldn't be fighting. Put down your sword. *(aside)* Not like you know what to do with it anyway. I do but keep the peace.

TYBALT: What! Drawn and talk of peace? I hate the word, as I hate hell, all Montagues, and thee. Have at thee coward!

(they fight; enter LORD/LADY CAPULET from one side of the stage; enter LORD/LADY MONTAGUE from the other side of the stage)

LORD/LADY CAPULET: My sword, I say! Old Montague is come.

LORD/LADY MONTAGUE: Thou villain Capulet! Hold me not, let me go.

(Lord/Ladies start to fight; PRINCE enters)

PRINCE: Rebellious subjects, enemies to peace. Will they not hear? *(as loud as possible)* STOP!!!!!! *(they all stop and go to their appropriate side)* This is the third time this year you have caused a riot on MY streets, and I am really getting tired of it. If ever you disturb our streets again, your lives shall pay the forfeit of the peace. Clear?

ALL: Clear.

TYBALT: Ahhhh, sorry but it's not clear to me, and probably not clear to them. *(points at audience)* I don't understand.

PRINCE: If you start a fight again, I will kill you – Clear? *(TYBALT nods)* Good, now, on pain of death, all men depart. *(no one leaves)* Go!

(ALL exit except BENVOLIO, LORD/LADY MONTAGUE)

LORD/LADY MONTAGUE: Benvolio, have you seen Romeo lately?

BENVOLIO: No, my friend has been avoiding me.

LORD/LADY MONTAGUE: He has been acting rather strange lately. Find out what is wrong with him, OK?

BENVOLIO: Will do!

(LORD/LADY MONTAGUE exit; ROMEO enters)

BENVOLIO: Romeo, Romeo!

ROMEO: Benvolio, there is this really cool girl, Rosaline, I mean, she's cute! Anyway, I like her a lot. But she wants nothing to do with me, what do I do?

BENVOLIO: Don't worry about her, there are other fish in the sea.

ROMEO: Yeah, whatever. Then teach me how I should forget to think. But hey, I hear she is going to a big party tonight, should we go?

BENVOLIO: Yes, and I will show you other girls more beautiful than she. Like her! Right there in the audience! *(points at audience member)* And I will make thee think thy swan a crow.

ROMEO: You're on!

(ALL exit)

ACT 1 SCENE 2

(enter LORD/LADY CAPULET and PARIS)

PARIS: Lord Capulet, I like your daughter, Juliet, can I marry her?

LORD/LADY CAPULET: Paris, buddy, listen, my daughter is only 13. She can't even drive yet! Why don't you wait about two more years and then we will talk.

PARIS: Pleeeeeeease. Pretty please.

LORD/LADY CAPULET: Hmmm. Well, I am having this really cool party tonight. Why don't you come, and if Juliet likes you and says yes, then, why not!

PARIS: Awesome!

(ALL exit)

ACT 1 SCENE 3

(enter LORD/LADY CAPULET, NURSE, JULIET)

LORD/LADY CAPULET: Juliet, my daughter, I hear that Paris thinks you are really cute.

NURSE: I have been your nurse all your life Juliet, and I believe you should think about this guy.

LORD/LADY CAPULET: Have you thought about marriage yet, because he is very good looking.

JULIET: If I like him, I will think about it.

NURSE: Great! Hey, let's go to the party!

(ALL exit)

ACT 1 SCENE 4

(enter ROMEO, MERCUTIO, BENVOLIO wearing masks)

BENVOLIO: Mercutio, are you sure that by wearing these masks we will be safe at a Capulet party?

MERCUTIO: No problem, they will have no clue.

ROMEO: Well here we are. But I don't see Rosaline.

BENVOLIO: I told you, look at the other girls.

ROMEO: Yeah, yeah.

MERCUTIO: You need to laugh my friend, if love be rough with you; be rough with love.

ROMEO: Leave me alone.

(enter LORD/LADY CAPULET, JULIET, TYBALT, NURSE, and other maskers all dancing and having a fun time)

ROMEO: *(seeing Juliet for the first time)* What lady is that which doth enrich the hand of yonder knight?

MERCUTIO: No clue, man.

ROMEO: *(to himself)* O she doth teach the torches to burn bright!

TYBALT: *(noticing Romeo)* What a Montague in the house of Capulet?

LORD/LADY CAPULET: Tybalt, don't pick a fight tonight.

TYBALT: What?! Aghhhh.... I will get him later. *(TYBALT exits)*

ROMEO: *(to Juliet)* Hey you're cute.

JULIET: So are you.

NURSE: Juliet, your mother wants to talk with you.

ROMEO: Who is her mother?

NURSE: Lady Capulet.

ROMEO: *(very dramatic to audience)* Oh nooooo. My mom is going to be bummed. I just fell in love with a Capulet.

(ALL exit except JULIET and NURSE)

JULIET: Nurse, who was that?

NURSE: Romeo, a Montague.

JULIET: *(very dramatic to audience)* Uh oh, that's trouble. I just fell in love with a Montague.

(ALL exit)

ACT 2 SCENE 1

(enter ROMEO and JULIET)

ROMEO: *(seeing JULIET)* But, soft! What light through yonder window breaks? It is the east, and Juliet is the sun.

JULIET: Ay me!

ROMEO: *(overwhelmed by her words)* She speaks! O speak again, bright angel!

JULIET: O Romeo, Romeo! Wherefore art thou Romeo? Deny thy father and refuse thy name; Or if thou wilt not, be but sworn my love, and I'll no longer be a Capulet. What's in a name? That which we call a rose by any other name would smell as sweet.

ROMEO: *(aside)* She is my sworn enemy, but look at her, WOW she's cute! See, how she leans her cheek upon her hand! O that I were a glove upon that hand, that I might touch that cheek! *(ROMEO is in a daze)*

JULIET: O Romeo, Romeo! Hello! HEY ROMEO!

ROMEO: Oh yeah, sorry, just daydreaming over here. Hey, I love you.

JULIET: And I love you.

ROMEO: I got an idea, let's get married.

JULIET: Okay. I will send my nurse tomorrow to find the time and place of our marriage.

ROMEO: Cool.

NURSE: *(offstage)* Juliet!

JULIET: Good night, Good night! Parting is such sweet sorrow, that I shall say good night till it be morrow.

(JULIET exits)

ROMEO: I need to go talk to Friar Lawrence to figure out this marriage thing.

(ROMEO exits)

ACT 2 SCENE 2

(enter FRIAR LAWRENCE)

FRIAR LAWRENCE: Ah, what a beautiful morning. *(picks up a plant and pricks his finger)* Ouch! Plants, like people, can be both good and evil.

(enter ROMEO)

FRIAR LAWRENCE: Romeo, what brings you here today?

ROMEO: I have a small request, and it's just slightly complicated. *(pauses)* I want to get married to Juliet.

FRIAR LAWRENCE: *(outraged)* The Capulet!

ROMEO: Yeah.

FRIAR LAWRENCE: *(still outraged)* Are you crazy!

ROMEO: But I am in love.

FRIAR LAWRENCE: *(very calm)* Well, okay. This might end the feud between the Montagues and the Capulets.

ROMEO: Awesome!

(ALL exit)

ACT 2 SCENE 3

(enter MERCUTIO and BENVOLIO)

BENVOLIO: Mercutio, have you seen Romeo since last night's party?

MERCUTIO: *(joking)* He's probably still in love with Rosaline.

(ROMEO enters)

ROMEO: Hey guys!

MERCUTIO: *(teasing Romeo)* Still in love with Rosaline?

ROMEO: Well, now that you mention it ...

(enter NURSE)

NURSE: So what's the plan?

MERCUTIO: *(very sarcastic)* Hey Romeo, now she's better than Rosaline.

NURSE: *(to Romeo)* What saucy merchant was this, that was so full of himself?

ROMEO: Ignore him, he's just a gentleman that LOVES to hear himself talk. Tell Juliet we will get married this afternoon at Friar Lawrence's.

NURSE: *Okay.*

(ALL exit)

ACT 2 SCENE 4

(enter FRIAR LAWRENCE, ROMEO, JULIET)

JULIET: My Nurse told me to meet you here to be married.

FRIAR LAWRENCE: Are you ready?

ROMEO: Ready.

JULIET: Ready.

FRIAR LAWRENCE: Okay, all done, you're married. You can now kiss the bride.

(ROMEO and JULIET look at each other and then towards FRIAR LAWRENCE shaking their heads 'no')

FRIAR LAWRENCE: Okay, fine, you can hug.

(ROMEO and JULIET look at each other and then towards FRIAR LAWRENCE shaking their heads 'no')

FRIAR LAWRENCE: Okay, okay. Can you at least shake hands?

(ROMEO and JULIET look at each other and decide to high five instead)

FRIAR LAWRENCE: *(to audience)* They just got married! Let's hear it for them!

(FRIAR gets audience to clap; ALL exit)

ACT 3 SCENE 1

(enter BENVOLIO and MERCUTIO; enter TYBALT from opposite side)

TYBALT: *(angry)* Where's Romeo?

MERCUTIO: You want some of me?

TYBALT: No, I want Romeo.

(enter ROMEO)

ROMEO: My good friends.

TYBALT: Bring it on, Romeo. Thou art a villain.

ROMEO: I will not fight you.

MERCUTIO: *(wanting to fight)* Come on Romeo.

ROMEO: No, I have my reasons.

BENVOLIO: We should listen to Romeo.

MERCUTIO: Fine, I'll fight him.

TYBALT: Let's go!

(MERCUTIO and TYBALT fight)

ROMEO: NO!

(TYBALT stabs MERCUTIO)

ROMEO: Good Mercutio!

MERCUTIO: A plague o' both your houses. I am sped.

(MERCUTIO dies)

ROMEO: Noooooooooooo, Mercutio! Aghhh....Tybalt, I'm really upset, I mean really, REALLY upset. *(pulling his sword out)*

BENVOLIO: Whoa, Romeo. Do you see that guy? *(pointing at dead MERCUTIO)* Do you want to be like him?

TYBALT: Oh yeah!

ROMEO: Yeah!

(ROMEO and TYBALT fight, TYBALT is killed)

BENVOLIO: Romeo, away, be gone!

(ROMEO exits; enter PRINCE, LORD/LADY CAPULET and MONTAGUE)

PRINCE: What in the world happened here? Why are there dead bodies on the ground all over MY streets? Huh?

BENVOLIO: Well, Tybalt killed Mercutio, and then Romeo killed Tybalt.

PRINCE: Fine, then Romeo is banished from Verona, and clean up this mess!

(BENVOLIO drags bodies off stage; ALL exit)

ACT 3 SCENE 2

(enter ROMEO and FRIAR LAWRENCE)

ROMEO: Friar, I did a bad thing.

FRIAR LAWRENCE: Yeah, I heard, not too good of you. The prince says you are to be banished from the kingdom.

ROMEO: Noooooooooooooo! I will never be able to see my Juliet again!

(ROMEO falls on the ground crying, very melodramatic; NURSE enters)

NURSE: Friar, have you seen Romeo?

(FRIAR points to the ground)

NURSE: Oh, yeah, pretty obvious and a bit pathetic. Hey lover boy. Juliet is pretty bummed.

ROMEO: Noooooooooooooo!

(ROMEO tries to stab himself, failing miserably; NURSE takes sword away)

FRIAR LAWRENCE: Why don't you go see Juliet, and then leave town.

ROMEO: *(excited)* Great idea!

(ALL exit)

ACT 4 SCENE 1

(enter ROMEO and JULIET)

JULIET: Oh Romeo!

ROMEO: Oh Juliet! It is almost morning, and I must leave.

JULIET: Do you have to?

ROMEO: I must be gone and live, or stay and die. And I really prefer the going and living thing.

(NURSE enters)

NURSE: Whoa, you're still here, you better leave soon, and when I say "soon" I mean, NOW!

(NURSE shoves out ROMEO; ROMEO exits and LORD/LADY CAPULET enter)

LORD/LADY CAPULET: Oh, by the way, Juliet, you have to marry Paris.

JULIET: I don't want to.

LORD/LADY CAPULET: What! You will do what I say!

JULIET: Fine!

(ALL exit but JULIET)

JULIET: I need to talk with Friar Lawrence.

(enter FRIAR LAWRENCE)

FRIAR LAWRENCE: You called?

JULIET: I want to stay with Romeo, what can I do?

FRIAR LAWRENCE: No problem. Just take this herbal cocktail. You will look like you are dead. And when they take you to the morgue, your Romeo will be there waiting. *(calling offstage)* Friar John!

(FRIAR JOHN enters)

FRIAR JOHN: Yes.

FRIAR LAWRENCE: I need you to send a message to Romeo.

FRIAR JOHN: Okay.

(FRIAR JOHN exits)

FRIAR LAWRENCE: *(calling offstage)* FRIAR JOHN!

(FRIAR JOHN enters)

FRIAR JOHN: Yes?

FRIAR LAWRENCE: You don't know what the message is.

FRIAR JOHN: Oh. Well, what is it?

FRIAR LAWRENCE: Tell Romeo to meet Juliet at the tomb tomorrow evening.

FRIAR JOHN: Okay.

(FRIAR JOHN exits)

FRIAR LAWRENCE: Good luck.

(FRIAR LAWRENCE exits)

JULIET: To drink, or not to drink, that is the question. Well, bottoms up!

(JULIET drinks potion, and passes out; NURSE enters)

NURSE: Rise and shine my dear. Juliet? Wake up. JULIET! NOOOOOOO.

(LORD/LADY CAPULET, FRIAR LAWRENCE, and PARIS enter)

ALL: Aghhhhh....

LORD/LADY CAPULET: My daughter!

FRIAR LAWRENCE: *(to himself)* Wow, that was quick.

LORD/LADY CAPULET: What?

FRIAR LAWRENCE: *(badly faking a cough)* I said, I feel sick. Now we need to take her to the tomb.

(they pick up JULIET, and carry her off stage, ALL exit)

ACT 5 SCENE 1

(enter ROMEO and BALTHASAR)

ROMEO: *(very happy)* Balthasar my servant, the day is beautiful! How are you today?

BALTHASAR: Ummm, okay.

ROMEO: Only okay, but the day is beautiful!

BALTHASAR: Well sir, ummmm I have bad news. Really bad news.

ROMEO: Really, no good news?

BALTHASAR: Nope.

ROMEO: Not even just a little.

BALTHASAR: Nope, nada, and no.

ROMEO: What's the bad news?

BALTHASAR: Juliet is dead.

ROMEO: NOOOOOOO......I am going to get some poison and kill myself tonight in her tomb.

(ALL exit)

(enter FRIAR JOHN and FRIAR LAWRENCE)

FRIAR LAWRENCE: Hello Friar John, were you able to deliver the letter? What says Romeo?

FRIAR JOHN: Well, I tried, but it just didn't happen, so I got a burger and fries instead, want one?

FRIAR LAWRENCE: What! That's not good. Bad, very bad. Poor Juliet, closed in a dead man's tomb. I have to go save them!

(ALL exit)

ACT 5 SCENE 3

(JULIET is lying dead on the ground, enter ROMEO)

ROMEO: I will open her tomb and kill myself next to my dear love Juliet!

(enter PARIS)

PARIS: My dear Romeo Montague, what are you doing here, disturbing a Capulet? I am putting you under arrest!

ROMEO: This is a bad time Paris. Tempt not a desperate man.

(they fight; ROMEO kills PARIS)

ROMEO: O Juliet, how I love you so. Here's to my love! *(Drinks poison)* Hmmmm, tastes like soda. *(or drink of choice)* Thus with a kiss I die.

(ROMEO dies; enter FRIAR LAWRENCE)

FRIAR LAWRENCE: Oh shoot, I am too late.

(JULIET awakes)

JULIET: O comfortable Friar, where is my lord?

FRIAR LAWRENCE: Yeah, well there was a slight problem with the plan. *(points at ground)*

JULIET: NOOOOOOOOOO!

FRIAR LAWRENCE: *(noises heard offstage)* I hear people coming, let's go!

(FRIAR LAWRENCE exits)

JULIET: No! What's here? Poison I see hath been his timeless end. Bummer, he left none for me. *(more noises outside)* Then I'll be brief. O happy dagger...

(ROMEO hands dagger to JULIET)

JULIET: Thank you. O happy dagger, this is thy sheath; there rest, and let me die.

(JULIET dies and falls on ROMEO; enter PRINCE, LORD/ LADY CAPULET, LORD/LADY MONTAGUE, and FRIAR LAWRENCE)

PRINCE: What misadventure is so early up? Why are there MORE dead bodies on MY streets?!

LORD/LADY CAPULET: My daughter is dead.

LORD/LADY MONTAGUE: My son too.

PRINCE: I will investigate and find out what happened here!

FRIAR LAWRENCE: I think I might know.

PRINCE: Tell us or die!

FRIAR LAWRENCE: Whoa! Okay, okay..... you see she liked him, he liked her, they got married.

LORD/LADY CAPULET and LORD/LADY MONTAGUE: WHAT!!!

FRIAR LAWRENCE: Anyway, they got married, Juliet faked dying; Romeo didn't know, that was the one thing that went wrong, and killed himself over her loss; she found out and killed herself over her loss of him. And now we stand here over the dead bodies.

PRINCE: *(to the LORDS/LADYS)* I want you to see what your quarreling has accomplished. Your two children are dead.

LORD/LADY CAPULET: Wow, I was wrong to act this way the entire time.

LORD/LADY MONTAGUE: Me too. Let's be friends! *(they hug)*

PRINCE: For never was a story of more woe, than this of Juliet and her Romeo.

(ALL exit)

THE END

The 25-Minute or so Romeo & Juliet

By William Shakespeare
Creatively modified by
Brendan P. Kelso

14-18+ Actors

THE CAPULETS

LORD CAPULET – Dad Capulet
LADY CAPULET – Mom Capulet
JULIET – The Babe (but a Capulet)
NURSE – Juliet's lifelong Nurse
[4]**TYBALT** – Juliet's cousin
[3]**SAMPSON** – Servant to Capulet
[1]**GREGORY** – Servant to Capulet

THE MONTAGUES

LORD MONTAGUE – Dad Montague
LADY MONTAGUE – Mom Montague
ROMEO – The Dude (but a Montague)
BENVOLIO – Romeo's friend
[2]**ABRAM** – Montague's servant
[4]**BALTHASAR** – Romeo's servant

THE COURT

PRINCE ESCALES – the local Prince
[3]**MERCUTIO** – Romeo's friend
[1]**PARIS** – Wants to marry Juliet

THE CHURCH

FRIAR LAWRENCE – A friar that helps
[2]**FRIAR JOHN** – A friar that doesn't help

The same actors can play the following parts:

[1]PARIS and GREGORY
[2]FRIAR JOHN and ABRAM
[3]MERCUTIO and SAMPSON
[4]TYBALT and BALTHASAR

If you are in the lucky position to have even more than 18 actors the rest can play various non-speaking roles such as: townsfolk, trees, pets of characters, etc. Basically, be creative!

PROLOGUE

(Montagues enter on one side of stage and face audience in a line and say, "Montagues" then they stand back; Capulets enter from the other side of the stage and say, "Capulets" then they stand back; they briefly glare, growl, and yell at each other; they then form a semi-circle and address the audience)

ROMEO: Two households, both alike in dignity,

JULIET: In fair Verona, where we lay our scene,

PARIS: From ancient grudge break to new mutiny,

FRIAR LAWRENCE: Where civil blood makes civil hands unclean.

FRIAR JOHN: From forth the fatal loins of these two foes

PRINCE: A pair of star-cross'd lovers take their life

MERCUTIO: Whose misadventured piteous overthrows

NURSE: Doth with their death bury their parents' strife.

TYBALT: The fearful passage of their death-marked love,

LORD CAPULET: And the continuance of their parents' rage,

LADY CAPULET: Which but their children's end, nought could remove,

LORD MONTAGUE: Is now the two hours', achmmm....25 minutes', traffic of our stage;

LADY MONTAGUE: The which if you with patient ears attend,

PRINCE: What here shall miss, our toil shall strive to mend.

(ALL exit)

ACT 1 SCENE 1

(enter SAMPSON and GREGORY)

SAMPSON: I really don't like those Montagues.

GREGORY: Yeah, we are so much better then they are.

(enter ABRAM, not noticing the other two)

SAMPSON: Hey look, a Montague. Go beat him up.

GREGORY: Okay. Hey you! Yeah, you ugly....ahhh...I mean Montague.

ABRAM: Capulets! You don't know when to stop, do you? Do you bite your thumb at me, sir?

SAMPSON: I do bite my thumb, sir. Bring it on!

(they are about to fight when BENVOLIO enters)

BENVOLIO: Whoa, hey guys, we really shouldn't be fighting. Put down your swords. *(aside)* Not like you know what to do with them anyway.

GREGORY: Oh look, another Montague.

(enter TYBALT)

SAMPSON: Hey Tybalt, the Montagues don't want to fight. They're babies!

TYBALT: What? A Montague? You want to fight! Let's go!

(wanting to fight)

BENVOLIO: *(drawing his sword)* Guys, we really shouldn't be fighting. I do but keep the peace.

TYBALT: What! Drawn and talk of peace? I hate the word, as I hate hell, all Montagues, and thee. Have at thee coward!

(they fight; enter LADY and LORD CAPULET from one side of the stage; enter LADY and LORD MONTAGUE from the other side of the stage)

LORD CAPULET: My sword, I say! Old Montague is come.

LADY CAPULET: Go get them, dear!

LORD MONTAGUE: Thou villain Capulet! Hold me not, let me go.

LADY MONTAGUE: *(to LADY CAPULET)* You want some of me!

(LORDS and LADIES start to fight; PRINCE enters)

PRINCE: Rebellious subjects, enemies to peace. Will they not hear? *(as loud as possible)* STOP!!!!!! *(they all stop and go to their appropriate side)* This is the third time this year you have caused a riot on MY streets, and I am really getting tired of it. If ever you disturb our streets again, your lives shall pay the forfeit of the peace. Clear?

ALL: Clear.

TYBALT: Ahhhh, sorry but it's not clear to me, and probably not clear to them. *(points at audience)* I don't understand.

PRINCE: If you start a fight again, I will kill you – Clear? *(TYBALT nods)* Good, now, on pain of death, all men depart. *(no one leaves)* Go!

(ALL exit except BENVOLIO, LORD and LADY MONTAGUE)

LADY MONTAGUE: Benvolio, have you seen Romeo lately?

BENVOLIO: No, Lord and Lady Montague, my friend has been avoiding me.

LORD MONTAGUE: He has been acting rather strange lately.

LADY MONTAGUE: Find out what is wrong with him, OK?

BENVOLIO: Will do!

(LORD and LADY MONTAGUE exit; ROMEO enters)

BENVOLIO: Romeo, Romeo!

ROMEO: Benvolio, there is this really cool girl, Rosaline, I mean, she's cute! Anyway, I like her a lot. But she wants nothing to do with me, what do I do?

BENVOLIO: Don't worry about her, there are other fish in the sea.

ROMEO: Yeah, whatever. Then teach me how I should forget to think. But hey, I hear she is going to a big party tonight, should we go?

BENVOLIO: Yes, and I will show you other girls more beautiful than she. Like her! Right there in the audience! *(points at audience member)* And I will make thee think thy swan a crow.

ROMEO: You're on!

(ALL exit)

ACT 1 SCENE 2

(enter LORD CAPULET and PARIS)

PARIS: Lord Capulet, I like your daughter, Juliet, can I marry her?

LORD CAPULET: Paris, buddy, listen, my daughter is only 13. She can't even drive yet! Why don't you wait about two more years and then we will talk.

PARIS: Pleeeeeeease. Pretty please.

LORD CAPULET: Hmmm. Well, I am having this really cool party tonight. Why don't you come, and if Juliet likes you and says yes, then, why not!

PARIS: Awesome!

(ALL exit)

(enter LADY CAPULET, NURSE, JULIET)

LADY CAPULET: Juliet, my daughter, I hear that Paris thinks you are really cute.

NURSE: I have been your nurse all your life Juliet, and I believe you should think about this guy.

LADY CAPULET: Have you thought about marriage yet, because he is very good looking.

JULIET: If I like him, I will think about it.

NURSE: Hey, let's go to the party!

(ALL exit)

ACT 1 SCENE 4

(enter ROMEO, MERCUTIO, BENVOLIO wearing masks)

BENVOLIO: Mercutio, are you sure that by wearing these masks we will be safe at a Capulet party?

MERCUTIO: No problem, they will have no clue.

ROMEO: Well here we are. But I don't see Rosaline.

BENVOLIO: I told you, look at the other girls.

ROMEO: Yeah, yeah.

MERCUTIO: You need to laugh my friend, if love be rough with you; be rough with love.

ROMEO: Leave me alone.

(enter LORD and LADY CAPULET, JULIET, TYBALT, NURSE, and other maskers all dancing and having a fun time)

ROMEO: *(seeing Juliet for the first time)* What lady is that which doth enrich the hand of yonder knight?

MERCUTIO: No clue, man.

ROMEO: *(to himself)* O she doth teach the torches to burn bright!

TYBALT: *(noticing Romeo)* What a Montague in the house of Capulet?

LORD CAPULET: Tybalt, don't pick a fight tonight.

TYBALT: What?! Aghhhh.... I will get him later. *(TYBALT exits)*

ROMEO: *(to Juliet)* Hey you're cute.

JULIET: So are you.

NURSE: Juliet, your mother wants to talk with you.

ROMEO: Who is her mother?

NURSE: Lady Capulet.

ROMEO: *(very dramatic to audience)* Oh nooooo. My mom is going to be bummed. I just fell in love with a Capulet.

(ALL exit except JULIET and NURSE)

JULIET: Nurse, who was that?

NURSE: Romeo, a Montague.

JULIET: *(very dramatic to audience)* Uh oh, that's trouble. I just fell in love with a Montague.

(ALL exit)

(enter ROMEO and JULIET)

ROMEO: *(seeing JULIET)* But, soft! What light through yonder window breaks? It is the east, and Juliet is the sun.

JULIET: Ay me!

ROMEO: *(overwhelmed by her words)* She speaks! O speak again, bright angel!

JULIET: O Romeo, Romeo! Wherefore art thou Romeo? Deny thy father and refuse thy name; Or if thou wilt not, be but sworn my love, and I'll no longer be a Capulet. What's in a name? That which we call a rose by any other name would smell as sweet.

ROMEO: *(aside)* She is my sworn enemy, but look at her, WOW she's cute! See, how she leans her cheek upon her hand! O that I were a glove upon that hand, that I might touch that cheek! *(ROMEO is in a daze)*

JULIET: O Romeo, Romeo! Hello! HEY ROMEO!

ROMEO: Oh yeah, sorry, just daydreaming over here. Hey, I love you.

JULIET: And I love you.

ROMEO: I got an idea, let's get married.

JULIET: Okay. I will send my nurse tomorrow to find the time and place of our marriage.

ROMEO: Cool.

NURSE: *(offstage)* Juliet!

JULIET: Good night, Good night! Parting is such sweet sorrow, that I shall say good night till it be morrow.

(JULIET exits)

ROMEO: I need to go talk to Friar Lawrence to figure out this marriage thing.

(ROMEO exits)

ACT 2 SCENE 2

(enter FRIAR LAWRENCE)

FRIAR LAWRENCE: Ah, what a beautiful morning. *(picks up a plant and pricks his finger)* Ouch! Plants, like people, can be both good and evil.

(enter ROMEO)

FRIAR LAWRENCE: Romeo, what brings you here today?

ROMEO: I have a small request, and it's just slightly complicated. *(pauses)* I want to get married to Juliet.

FRIAR LAWRENCE: *(outraged)* The Capulet!

ROMEO: Yeah.

FRIAR LAWRENCE: *(still outraged)* Are you crazy!

ROMEO: But I am in love.

FRIAR LAWRENCE: *(very calm)* Well, okay. This might end the feud between the Montagues and the Capulets.

ROMEO: Awesome!

(ALL exit)

(enter MERCUTIO and BENVOLIO)

BENVOLIO: Mercutio, have you seen Romeo since last night's party?

MERCUTIO: *(joking)* He's probably still in love with Rosaline.

(ROMEO enters)

ROMEO: Hey guys!

MERCUTIO: *(teasing Romeo)* Still in love with Rosaline?

ROMEO: Well, now that you mention it ...

(enter NURSE)

NURSE: So what's the plan?

MERCUTIO: *(very sarcastic)* Hey Romeo, now she's better than Rosaline.

NURSE: *(to Romeo)* What saucy merchant was this, that was so full of himself?

ROMEO: Ignore him, he's just a gentleman that LOVES to hear himself talk. Tell Juliet we will get married this afternoon at Friar Lawrence's.

NURSE: Okay.

(ALL exit)

ACT 2 SCENE 4

(enter FRIAR LAWRENCE, ROMEO, JULIET)

JULIET: My Nurse told me to meet you here to be married.

FRIAR LAWRENCE: Are you ready?

ROMEO: Ready.

JULIET: Ready.

FRIAR LAWRENCE: Okay, all done, you're married. You can now kiss the bride.

(ROMEO and JULIET look at each other and then towards FRIAR LAWRENCE shaking their heads 'no')

FRIAR LAWRENCE: Okay, fine, you can hug.

(ROMEO and JULIET look at each other and then towards FRIAR LAWRENCE shaking their heads 'no')

FRIAR LAWRENCE: Okay, okay. Can you at least shake hands?

(ROMEO and JULIET look at each other and decide to high five instead)

FRIAR LAWRENCE: *(to audience)* They just got married! Let's hear it for them!

(FRIAR gets audience to clap; ALL exit)

ACT 3 SCENE 1

(enter BENVOLIO and MERCUTIO; enter TYBALT from opposite side)

TYBALT: *(angry)* Where's Romeo?

MERCUTIO: You want some of me?

TYBALT: No, I want Romeo.

(enter ROMEO)

ROMEO: My good friends.

TYBALT: Bring it on, Romeo. Thou art a villain.

ROMEO: I will not fight you.

MERCUTIO: *(wanting to fight)* Come on Romeo.

ROMEO: No, I have my reasons.

BENVOLIO: We should listen to Romeo.

MERCUTIO: Fine, I'll fight him.

TYBALT: Let's go!

(MERCUTIO and TYBALT fight)

ROMEO: NO!

(TYBALT stabs MERCUTIO)

ROMEO: Good Mercutio!

MERCUTIO: A plague o' both your houses. I am sped.

(MERCUTIO dies)

ROMEO: Noooooooooooo, Mercutio! Aghhh....Tybalt, I'm really upset, I mean really, REALLY upset. *(pulling his sword out)*

BENVOLIO: Whoa, Romeo. Do you see that guy? *(pointing at dead MERCUTIO)* Do you want to be like him?

TYBALT: Oh yeah!

ROMEO: Yeah!

(ROMEO and TYBALT fight, TYBALT is killed)

BENVOLIO: Romeo, away, be gone!

(ROMEO exits; enter PRINCE, LORD and LADY CAPULET and MONTAGUE)

PRINCE: What in the world happened here? Why are there dead bodies on the ground all over MY streets? Huh?

BENVOLIO: Well, Tybalt killed Mercutio, and then Romeo killed Tybalt.

PRINCE: Fine, then Romeo is banished from Verona, and clean up this mess!

(ALL exit; BENVOLIO drags bodies off stage)

ACT 3 SCENE 2

(enter ROMEO and FRIAR LAWRENCE)

ROMEO: Friar, I did a bad thing.

FRIAR LAWRENCE: Yeah, I heard, not too good of you. The prince says you are to be banished from the kingdom.

ROMEO: Noooooooooooooo! I will never be able to see my Juliet again!

(ROMEO falls on the ground crying, very melodramatic; NURSE enters)

NURSE: Friar, have you seen Romeo?

(FRIAR points to the ground)

NURSE: Oh, yeah, pretty obvious and a bit pathetic. Hey lover boy. Juliet is pretty bummed.

ROMEO: Noooooooooooooo!

(ROMEO tries to stab himself, failing miserably; NURSE takes sword away)

FRIAR LAWRENCE: Why don't you go see Juliet, and then leave town.

ROMEO: *(excited)* Great idea!

(ALL exit)

ACT 4 SCENE 1

(enter ROMEO and JULIET)

JULIET: Oh Romeo!

ROMEO: Oh Juliet! It is almost morning, and I must leave.

JULIET: Do you have to?

ROMEO: I must be gone and live, or stay and die. And I really prefer the going and living thing.

(NURSE enters)

NURSE: Whoa, you're still here, you better leave soon, and when I say "soon" I mean, NOW!

(NURSE shoves out ROMEO; ROMEO exits and LADY and LORD CAPULET enter)

LADY CAPULET: Oh, by the way, Juliet, your dad says you have to marry Paris.

JULIET: I don't want to.

LORD CAPULET: What! You will do what I say!

JULIET: Fine!

(ALL exit but JULIET)

JULIET: I need to talk with Friar Lawrence.

(enter FRIAR LAWRENCE)

FRIAR LAWRENCE: You called?

JULIET: I want to stay with Romeo, what can I do?

FRIAR LAWRENCE: No problem. Just take this herbal cocktail. You will look like you are dead. And when they take you to the morgue, your Romeo will be there waiting. *(calling offstage)* Friar John!

(FRIAR JOHN enters)

FRIAR JOHN: Yes.

FRIAR LAWRENCE: I need you to send a message to Romeo.

FRIAR JOHN: Okay.

(FRIAR JOHN exits)

FRIAR LAWRENCE: *(calling offstage)* FRIAR JOHN!

(FRIAR JOHN enters)

FRIAR JOHN: Yes?

FRIAR LAWRENCE: You don't know what the message is.

FRIAR JOHN: Oh. Well, what is it?

FRIAR LAWRENCE: Tell Romeo to meet Juliet at the tomb tomorrow evening.

FRIAR JOHN: Okay.

(FRIAR JOHN exits)

FRIAR LAWRENCE: Good luck.

(FRIAR LAWRENCE exits)

JULIET: To drink, or not to drink, that is the question. Well, bottoms up!

(JULIET drinks potion, and passes out; NURSE enters)

NURSE: Rise and shine my dear. Juliet? Wake up. JULIET! NOOOOOOO.

(LADY and LORD CAPULET, FRIAR LAWRENCE, and PARIS enter)

ALL: Aghhhhh....

LORD CAPULET: My daughter!

FRIAR LAWRENCE: *(to himself)* Wow, that was quick.

LORD CAPULET: What?

FRIAR LAWRENCE: *(badly faking a cough)* I said, I feel sick. Now we need to take her to the tomb.

(they pick up JULIET, and carry her off stage, ALL exit)

(enter ROMEO and BALTHASAR)

ROMEO: *(very happy)* Balthasar my servant, the day is beautiful! How are you today?

BALTHASAR: Ummm, okay.

ROMEO: Only okay, but the day is beautiful!

BALTHASAR: Well sir, ummmm I have bad news. Really bad news.

ROMEO: Really, no good news?

BALTHASAR: Nope.

ROMEO: Not even just a little.

BALTHASAR: Nope, nada, and no.

ROMEO: What's the bad news?

BALTHASAR: Juliet is dead.

ROMEO: NOOOOOOO......I am going to get some poison and kill myself tonight in her tomb.

(ALL exit)

ACT 5 SCENE 2

(enter FRIAR JOHN and FRIAR LAWRENCE)

FRIAR LAWRENCE: Hello Friar John, were you able to deliver the letter? What says Romeo?

FRIAR JOHN: Well, I tried, but it just didn't happen, so I got a burger and fries instead, want one?

FRIAR LAWRENCE: What! That's not good. Bad, very bad. Poor Juliet, closed in a dead man's tomb. I have to go save them!

(ALL exit)

(JULIET is lying dead on the ground, enter ROMEO)

ROMEO: I will open her tomb and kill myself next to my dear love Juliet!

(enter PARIS)

PARIS: My dear Romeo Montague, what are you doing here, disturbing a Capulet? I am putting you under arrest!

ROMEO: This is a bad time Paris. Tempt not a desperate man.

(they fight; ROMEO kills PARIS)

ROMEO: O Juliet, how I love you so. Here's to my love! *(Drinks poison)* Hmmmm, tastes like soda. *(or drink of choice)* Thus with a kiss I die.

(ROMEO dies; enter FRIAR LAWRENCE)

FRIAR LAWRENCE: Oh shoot, I am too late.

(JULIET awakes)

JULIET: O comfortable Friar, where is my lord?

FRIAR LAWRENCE: Yeah, well there was a slight problem with the plan. *(points at ground)*

JULIET: NOOOOOOOOOO!

FRIAR LAWRENCE: I hear people coming, let's go!

(FRIAR LAWRENCE exIts)

JULIET: What's here? Poison I see hath been his timeless end. Bummer, he left none for me. *(noises outside)* Then I'll be brief. O happy dagger...

(ROMEO hands dagger to JULIET)

JULIET: Thank you. O happy dagger, this is thy sheath; there rest, and let me die.

(JULIET dies and falls on ROMEO; enter PRINCE, LORD CAPULET, LORD MONTAGUE, and FRIAR LAWRENCE)

PRINCE: What misadventure is so early up? Why are there MORE dead bodies on MY streets?!

LORD CAPULET: My daughter is dead.

LORD MONTAGUE: My son too.

PRINCE: I will investigate and find out what happened here!

FRIAR LAWRENCE: I think I might know.

PRINCE: Tell us or die!

FRIAR LAWRENCE: Whoa! Okay, okay..... you see she liked him, he liked her, they got married.

LORD CAPULET and LORD MONTAGUE: WHAT!!!

FRIAR LAWRENCE: Anyway, they got married, Juliet faked dying; Romeo didn't know, that was the one thing that went wrong, and killed himself over her loss; she found out and killed herself over her loss of him. And now we stand here over the dead bodies.

PRINCE: *(to the LORDS)* I want you to see what your quarreling has accomplished. Your two children are dead.

LORD CAPULET: Wow, I was wrong to act this way the entire time.

LORD MONTAGUE: Me too. Let's be friends! *(they hug)*

PRINCE: For never was a story of more woe, than this of Juliet and her Romeo.

(ALL exit)

THE END

Sneak Peeks at other Playing With Plays books:

Oliver Twist
for Kids

(enter FAGIN, SIKES, DODGER and NANCY)

DODGER: So that Oliver kid got caught by the police.

FAGIN: He could tell them all our secrets and get us in trouble; we've got to find him. Like, in the next 30 seconds or so.

SIKES: Send Nancy. She's good at getting information quick.

NANCY: Nope. Don't wanna go, Sikes. I like the kid.

SIKES: She'll go, Fagin.

NANCY: No, she won't, Fagin.

SIKES: Yes, she will, Fagin.

NANCY: Fine! Grrrrr....

(NANCY sticks out her tongue at SIKES and storms offstage, then immediately returns)

NANCY: Okay, I checked with my sources and, some gentleman took him home to take care of him.

(NANCY, DODGER and SIKES stare at FAGIN waiting for direction)

FAGIN: Where?

NANCY: I don't know.

FAGIN: WHAT!?!? *(waiting)* Well don't just stand there, GO FIND HIM! *(to audience)* Can't find any good help these days!

(all run offstage, bumping into each other in their haste)

ACT 2 SCENE 2

(enter OLIVER)

OLIVER: *(to audience)* I'm out running an errand for Mr. Brownlow to prove that I'm a trustworthy boy. I can't keep hanging out with thieves, right?

(enter NANCY, who runs over to OLIVER and grabs him; SIKES, FAGIN, and DODGER enter shortly after and follow NANCY)

NANCY: Oh my dear brother! I've found him! Oh! Oliver! Oliver!

OLIVER: What!?!? I don't have a sister!

NANCY: You do now, kid. Let's go. *(she drags OLIVER to FAGIN)*

FAGIN: Dodger, take Oliver and lock him up.

DODGER: *(to OLIVER)* Sorry, dude. *(DODGER and OLIVER start to exit)*

OLIVER: Aw, man! Seriously? I just found a good home...

NANCY: Don't be too mean to him, Fagin.

OLIVER: *(as he's exiting)* Yeah, don't be too mean to me, Fagin!

SIKES: *(mimicking NANCY)* Don't be mean, Fagin. Wah, wah, wah. Look, I need Oliver to help me rob a house, okay? He is just the size I want to fit through the window. All sneaky ninja like.

Richard III for Kids

ACT 1 SCENE 4

(CLARENCE is in prison, sleeping; he wakes up from a bad dream)

CLARENCE: Terrible, horrible, no good, very bad dream! *(pauses, notices audience and addresses them)* O, I have pass'd a miserable night! I dreamt that Richard was trying to kill me! Hahahaha, Richard is SUCH a good guy, he would NEVER do a thing like that!

(enter MURDERER carrying a weapon)

MURDERER: I sounded like such a pro, no one will know it's my first day on the job! Hehehe!

CLARENCE: Hey! Who's there?

MURDERER: Um... um... *(hides his murder weapon behind his back)*

CLARENCE: Your eyes do menace me. Are you planning to murder me? 'Cause that's not a good idea. My brother Richard is a REALLY powerful guy.

MURDERER: Ha! Richard is the one who sent me here to do this! *(a pause)* Whoops...

CLARENCE: Hahaha, you foolish fellow. Richard loves me.

MURDERER: Dude, what are you not getting? He PAID me to do this!

CLARENCE: O, do not slander him, for he is kind.

(The MURDERER stabs CLARENCE; CLARENCE dies a dramatic death)

CLARENCE: Kinda ruthless... *(dies)*

MURDERER: *(Gasps)* Oh, my! He's dead! I feel bad now... I bet Clarence was a really nice guy. Ahhh, the guilt! Wow, I should have stayed in clown school.

(MURDERER exits)

ACT 2 SCENE 1

(KING EDWARD is surrounded by QUEEN ELIZABETH and BUCKINGHAM)

KING EDWARD: Well, this has been a great day at work! Everyone's agreed to get along!

(ELIZABETH and BUCKINGHAM shake hands with each other to celebrate the peace; enter RICHARD; KING EDWARD smiles happily)

KING EDWARD: If I die, I will be at peace! But I must say I'm feeling a lot healthier after all of this peace-making!

RICHARD: Hey! Looks like you're all in a good mood. That's great, 'cause you know I LOVE getting along! So what's up?

KING EDWARD: I made them like each other!

RICHARD: How lovely! I like you all now, too! Group hug? *(everyone shakes their head)* No? *(he grins sweetly)*

ELIZABETH: Wonderful! Once Clarence gets back from the Tower, everything will be perfect!

RICHARD: WHAT??? We make peace and then you insult us like this? That's no way to talk about a DEAD man!!

(EVERYONE gasps)

KING EDWARD: Is Clarence dead? I told them to cancel the execution!

RICHARD: Oh, yeah... guess that was too late! *(winks to audience)*

KING EDWARD: Nooooooo!!!! Oh my poor brother! Now I feel more sick than EVER! Oh, poor Clarence!

(ALL exit except RICHARD and BUCKINGHAM)

RICHARD: Well, that sure worked as planned!

BUCKINGHAM: Great job, partner!

(both exit, laughing evilly)

Treasure Island
for Kids

(enter JIM, TRELAWNEY, and DOCTOR; enter CAPTAIN SMOLLETT from the other side of the stage)

TRELAWNEY: Hello Captain. Are we all shipshape and seaworthy?

CAPTAIN: Trelawney, I don't know what you're thinking, but I don't like this cruise; and I don't like the men.

TRELAWNEY: *(very angry)* Perhaps you don't like the ship?

CAPTAIN: Nope, I said it short and sweet.

DOCTOR: What? Why?

CAPTAIN: Because I heard we are going on a treasure hunt and the coordinates of the island are: *(whispers to DOCTOR)*

DOCTOR: Wow! That's exactly right!

CAPTAIN: There's been too much blabbing already.

DOCTOR: Right! But, I doubt ANYTHING will go wrong!

CAPTAIN: Fine. Let's sail!

(ALL exit)

Act 2 Scene 3

(enter JIM, SILVER, and various other pirates)

SILVER: Ay, ay, mates. You know the song: Fifteen men on the dead man's chest.

ALL PIRATES: Yo-ho-ho and a bottle of rum!

(PIRATES slowly exit)

JIM: *(to the audience)* So, the Hispaniola had begun her voyage to the Isle of Treasure. As for Long John, well, he still is the nicest cook...

SILVER: Do you want a sandwich?

JIM: That would be great, thanks Long John! *(SILVER exits; JIM addresses audience)* As you can see, Long John is a swell guy! Until...

(JIM hides in the corner)

Act 2 Scene 4

(enter SILVER and OTHER PIRATES)

JIM: *(to audience)* I overheard Long John talking to the rest of the pirates.

SILVER: Listen here you, Scallywags! I was with Captain Flint when he hid this treasure. And those cowards have the map. Follow my directions, and no killing, yet. Clear?

DICK: Clear.

SILVER: But, when we do kill them, I claim Trelawney. And remember, dead men don't bite.

GEORGE: Ay, ay, Long John!

(ALL exit but JIM)

JIM: *(to audience)* Oh no! Long John Silver IS the one-legged man that Billy Bones warned me about! I have to tell the others!

(JIM runs offstage)

Henry V for Kids

ACT 2 SCENE 2

(enter BEDFORD and EXETER, observing CAMBRIDGE and SCROOP, who whisper among themselves)

BEDFORD: Hey Exeter, do you think it's a good idea that King Henry is letting those conspirators wander around freely?

EXETER: It's alright, Bedford. King Henry has a plan! He knows EVERYTHING they are plotting. BUT, they don't KNOW he knows. And HE knows that they don't know he knows...and...

BEDFORD: *(interrupting)* Okay, okay, I get it. Let's go sit in the audience and watch! *(they sit in the audience; enter HENRY)*

HENRY: Greetings, my good and FAITHFUL friends, Cambridge and Scroop. Perfect timing! I need your advice on something.

CAMBRIDGE: Sure thing. You know we'd do anything for you! Never was a monarch better feared and loved.

SCROOP: That's why we're going to kick some French butt!! *(SCROOP and CAMBRIDGE high-five)*

HENRY: Excellent! A man was arrested yesterday for shouting nasty things about me. But I'm sure by now he's thought better of it. I think I ought to show mercy and pardon him.

SCROOP: Nah, let him be punished.

HENRY: Ahhh, but let us yet be merciful.

CAMBRIDGE: Nah, I'm with Scroop! Off with his head!

HENRY: Is that your final answer?

CAMBRIDGE & SCROOP: YES!

HENRY: Ok, but if we don't show mercy for small offenses, how will we show mercy for big ones? I will release him. Now, take a look at THESE LETTERS.

(as CAMBRIDGE and SCROOP read the letters, their jaws drop)

HENRY: Why, how now, gentlemen? What see you in those papers that your jaws hang so low?

EXETER: *(to audience)* The letters betray their guilt!

CAMBRIDGE: I do confess my fault...

SCROOP:....and do submit me to your Highness' mercy! *(they start begging and pleading on the ground)*

HENRY: Exeter, Bedford, arrest these traitors. What did they say... Oh yeah, OFF WITH THEIR HEADS!

CAMBRIDGE: Whoa there!

SCROOP: Off with our what? What happened to the whole "mercy" thing you were just talking about!?

HENRY: Your own words talked me out of it! Take them away!

CAMBRIDGE: Well, this stinks!

(EXETER and BEDFORD arrest CAMBRIDGE and SCROOP; ALL exit, except HENRY)

HENRY: Being king is no fun sometimes. Scroop used to be one of my best friends. *(SCROOP runs on stage and dies melodramatically)* But there's no time to mope! *(CAMBRIDGE runs on stage and dies on top of SCROOP)* The signs of war advance. No king of England, if not King of France! NOW CLEAN UP THIS MESS!

(EXETER and BEDFORD run on stage and drag bodies off; exit HENRY)

King Lear for Kids

ACT 1 SCENE 1

KING LEAR's palace

(enter FOOL entertaining the audience with jokes, dancing, juggling, Hula Hooping... whatever the actor's skill may be; enter KENT)

KENT: Hey, Fool!

FOOL: What did you call me?!

KENT: I called you Fool.

FOOL: That's my name, don't wear it out! *(to audience)* Seriously, that's my name in the play!

(enter LEAR, CORNWALL, ALBANY, GONERIL, REGAN, and CORDELIA)

LEAR: The lords of France and Burgundy are outside. They both want to marry you, Cordelia.

ALL: Ooooooo!

LEAR: *(to audience)* Between you and me she IS my favorite child! *(to the girls)* Daughters, I need to talk to you about something. It's a really big deal.

GONERIL & REGAN: Did you buy us presents?

LEAR: This is even better than presents!

GONERIL & REGAN: Goody, goody!!!

CORDELIA: Father, your love is enough for me.

LEAR: Give me the map there, Kent. Girls, I'm tired. I've made a decision: Know that we - and by 'we' I mean 'me' - have divided in three our kingdom...

KENT: Whoa! Sir, dividing the kingdom may cause chaos! People could die!

FOOL: Well, this IS a tragedy...

LEAR: You worry too much, Kent. I'm giving it to my daughters so their husbands can be rich and powerful... like me!

CORNWALL & ALBANY: Sweet!

GONERIL & REGAN: Wait... what?

CORDELIA: This is olden times. That means that everything we own belongs to our husbands.

GONERIL & REGAN: Olden times stink!

CORDELIA: Truth.

LEAR: So, my daughters, tell your daddy how much you love him. Goneril, our eldest-born, speak first.

GONERIL: Sir, I love you more than words can say! More than outer space, puppies and cotton candy! I love you more than any child has ever loved a father in the history of the entire world, dearest Pops!

CORDELIA: *(to audience)* Holy moly! Surely, he won't be fooled by that. *(to self)* Love, and be silent.

LEAR: Thanks, sweetie! I'm giving you this big chunk of the kingdom here. What says our second daughter, Our dearest Regan, wife to Cornwall? Speak.

REGAN: What she said, Daddy... times a thousand!

CORDELIA: *(to audience)* What?! I love my father more than either of them. But I can't express it in words. My love's more richer than my tongue.

LEAR: Wow, Regan! You get this big hunk of the kingdom. Cordelia, what can you tell me to get this giant piece of kingdom as your own? Speak.

CORDELIA: Nothing, my lord.

LEAR: Nothing?!?

CORDELIA: Nothing.

LEAR: Come on, now. Nothing will come of nothing.

CORDELIA: I love you as a daughter loves her father.

LEAR: Try a little, harder, sweetie!

CORDELIA: Why are my sisters married if they give you all their love?

LEAR: How did you get so mean?

CORDELIA: Father, I will not insult you by telling you my love is like... as big as a whale.

LEAR: *(getting mad)* Fine. I'll split your share between your sisters.

REGAN, GONERIL, & CORNWALL: Yessss!

KENT: Whoa! Let's all just calm down a minute!

LEAR: Peace, Kent! You don't want to mess with me right now. I told you she was my favorite...

GONERIL & REGAN: What!?

LEAR: ...and she can't even tell me she loves me more than a whale? Nope. Now I'm mad.

KENT: Royal Lear, really...

LEAR: Kent, I'm pretty emotional right now! You better not try to talk me out of this...

KENT: Sir, you're acting ... insane.

Two Gentlemen of Verona
for Kids

ANTONIO: It's not nothing.

PROTEUS: Ahhhhh......It's a letter from Valentine, telling me what a great time he's having in Milan, yeah... that's what it says!

ANTONIO: Awesome! Glad to hear it! Because, you leave tomorrow to join Valentine in Milan.

PROTEUS: What!? Dad! No way! I don't want... I mean, I need some time. I've got some things to do.

ANTONIO: Like what?

PROTEUS: You know...things! Important things! And stuff! Lots of stuff!

ANTONIO: No more excuses! Go pack your bag. *(ANTONIO begins to exit)*

PROTEUS: Fie!

ANTONIO: What was that?

PROTEUS: Fiiii......ne with me, Pops! *(ANTONIO exits)* I was afraid to show my father Julia's letter, lest he should take exceptions to my love; and my own lie of an excuse made it easier for him to send me away.

ANTONIO: *(Offstage)* Proteus! Get a move on!!

PROTEUS: Fie!!!

(exit)

ACT 2 SCENE 1

(enter VALENTINE and SPEED following)

VALENTINE: Ah, Silvia, Silvia! *(heavy sighs)*

SPEED: *(mocking)* Madam Silvia! Madam Silvia! Gag me.

VALENTINE: Knock it off! You don't know her.

SPEED: Do too. She's the one that you can't stop staring at. Makes me wanna barf.

VALENTINE: I do not stare!

SPEED: You do. AND you keep singing that silly love song. *(sing INSERT SAPPY LOVE SONG)* You used to be so much fun.

VALENTINE: Huh? *(heavy sigh, starts humming SAME LOVE SONG)*

SPEED: Never mind.

VALENTINE: I have loved her ever since I saw her. Here she comes!

SPEED: Great. *(to audience)* Watch him turn into a fool.

(enter SILVIA)

VALENTINE: Hey, Silvia.

SILVIA: Hey, Valentine. What's goin' on?

VALENTINE: Nothin'. What's goin' on with you?

SILVIA: Nothin'.

(pause)

VALENTINE: What are you doing later?

SILVIA: Not sure. Prob-ly nothin'. You?

VALENTINE: Me neither. Nothin'.

SILVIA: Yea?

VALENTINE: Probably.

SPEED: *(to audience)* Kill me now.

SILVIA: Well, I guess I better go.

VALENTINE: Oh, okay! See ya'..

(pause)

SILVIA: See ya' later maybe?

VALENTINE: Oh, yea! Maybe! Yea! Okay!

SILVIA: Bye.

VALENTINE: Bye!

(exit SILVIA)

SPEED: *(aside)* Wow. *(to VALENTINE)* Dude, what the heck was that?

VALENTINE: I think she has a boyfriend. I can tell.

SPEED: Dude! She is so into you! How could you not see that?

VALENTINE: Do you think?

SPEED: Come on. We'll talk it through over dinner. *(to audience)* Fool. Am I right?

(exit)

BRENDAN P. KELSO, came to writing modified Shakespeare scripts when he was taking time off from work to be at home with his newly born son. "It just grew from there". Within months, he was being asked to offer classes in various locations and acting organizations along the Central Coast of California. Originally employed as an engineer, Brendan never thought about writing. However, his unique personality, humor, and love for engaging the kids with The Bard has led him to leave the engineering world and pursue writing as a new adventure in life! He has always believed, "the best way to learn is to have fun!" Brendan makes his home on the Central Coast of California and loves to spend time with his wife and son.

NOTES

Printed in Great
Britain
by Amazon